*An Inductive Study
of the Book of
Titus*

Sophron Studies
SOUND DOCTRINE... SOUND THINKING... SOUND LIVING

Preface

Welcome to the study of Titus! We are glad you're here. This is an inductive study of the book of Titus. If this method is unfamiliar to you, please do not become anxious as we will guide you through the process daily and weekly. You will study a portion of Scripture at a time, beginning with Titus 1:1, and will work through the end of Titus. This approach to study ensures proper context. Titus is one small part of sixty-six parts that make up God's word---you will see how Titus fits into all of Scripture.

This study is ideally intended to be done in a group setting, but can be done alone for personal Bible study. You are to complete each lesson individually, prior to attending your weekly group time. We suggest there be an appointed facilitator to guide your group through the questions (there is also a Leader's Guide Workbook available). The In-Class Worksheets included for some lessons are optional and intended to further your understanding of the passages just studied.

What is the goal of Bible study? To know God, to grow in the grace and knowledge of our Lord and Savior Jesus Christ (2 Peter 3:14), and to learn about our hope of eternal life (Titus 1:2). What will you get out of this study? That depends on you. Think of it as a sowing and reaping principle that can lead to sound doctrine, sound thinking, and sound living. Scripture is our source for growth as the Spirit leads.

It is our prayer that your roots will grow deep into God's love and His word. For roots to grow deep, there must be cultivation by hard work, tilling, pruning, watchfulness, and diligent sowing. To reap deep roots involves time, effort, and dependence on Almighty God! Be patient and enjoy your time with the Lord as you interact with Jesus Christ, the Word.

We would love to hear from you as you learn to study inductively and as you learn more about our Lord through Titus. Visit our website at **www.sophronstudies.com** and send us an email! Now, enjoy *Titus: For the Sake of The Faith*.

Blessings,
Melissa and Lisa

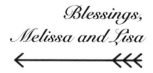

Contents

Sophron Studies

SOUND DOCTRINE... SOUND THINKING... SOUND LIVING

Sophron Studies is a reformed, inductive, in-depth approach to the study of God's word. *Sophron*, pronounced "so-fron," is the Greek word for a sound mind. It is curbing one's desires and impulses with self-control and temperance. As believers, we need to be women who study and delight in Him and His word, women who train to have a mind centered on God and renewed by truth (Romans 12:1–2).

A *sophron* mind is God's design for every believer. A *sophron* woman has a wise and sound mind and uses sound judgment; she cultivates prudence and exercises restraint over all her thoughts, whims, plans, passions, and pursuits of desire. A *sophron* woman trains to conform her mind to Jesus Christ: she is single-minded.

A woman who is not *sophron* could struggle with impure and irrational thoughts; she may allow her mind to wander without caution. The mindless woman becomes a forgetful hearer (James 1:25), is sluggish in her walk (Hebrews 6:12), and one who moves away from the hope of the gospel of our Lord Jesus Christ (Colossians 1:23).

Who is the *sophron* woman? Who is the woman who is not? It may be the same woman! If we are not training our thinking to be captivated with our Savior, we end up divided in our thinking, unstable and fearful. The sober minded woman can become unrestrained in her mind when she is angered or fearful. The *sophron* woman and the *unsophron* woman could indeed be the same woman.

Sophron Studies is designed to encourage you to stay focused on our only hope, Jesus Christ! Make it a habit to set your mind on the things above (Colossians 3:1–2). Study diligently to know Him through His word, to be a woman of a sound, *sophron* mind.

The Process of Study

S   Survey

Read prayerfully with purpose. Read to survey, or gain an overview; to lay the contextual foundation (per the lesson instruction). There are guided *surveys* throughout the study to aid your overview.

O   Observe

Observe only the basic facts by looking at specific questions in the lessons. Questions will guide you to consider: What is the context? Who is it about? Why? When did this happen? Why did that happen?

P   Particulars

To study the details of a given section of Scripture through interpretation by way of cross-references, lists, charts, and defining words in the original Greek or Hebrew language. (See "Lost in Translation" at the end of this study.)

H   Harmonize

Begin to better understand the harmony or context of the passage as the author intended. Begin also to connect parts of Scripture (2 Timothy 3:16—17). Context is crucial to understanding!

R   Reiterate

This is an important exercise which requires you to summarize what you have learned. To rewrite, recap, and recount what you have learned; to *own* the Scripture you study.

O   Obey

How does what you have learned affect you? Agree and accept God's Word as truth. How will you apply truth to your life? How will the author's message enable you to increase in your view of God? Sound doctrine will lead to sound thinking which will be evidenced in sound living. Obedience is application and application is obedience.

N   Nourishment

The word of God is the milk which we are to long for (1 Peter 2:2) and solid food for the mature who, because of practice, have their senses trained to discern good and evil (Hebrews 5:14). God's word nourishes your soul and progressively makes you more like Jesus Christ as you practice His word.

Before you begin...

Throughout the ten lessons of **For the Sake of The Faith: An Inductive Study of the book of Titus**, there will be numerous instructions directing you to annotate, color-code, and mark the text of Titus. Therefore, having your own printed copy of Titus will aid in a more effective study as you respond and interact with the word of God.

Please visit www.blueletterbible.org or www.biblegateway.com to print your own copy of the Titus text (chapters one through three), in the ESV for your personal use.

However, if you prefer, you may simply use your Bible and mark as you feel comfortable in doing so.

Book Survey

Lesson One: Titus 1-3

Let the words of my mouth and the meditation of my heart
be acceptable in your sight, O Lord, my rock and my redeemer.

—Psalm 19:14

Part One: First Impressions

This week's lesson is about observing the facts written in the letter to Titus, a *survey* to get an overview of the entire book. Read through your printed copy of Titus. Answer the following, using only the Titus text. Do not use other resources.

1. What are your first impressions?

2. What words are repeated?

3. Using only one word, summarize the letter to Titus.

4. Who is the author?

5. What are the themes throughout the three chapters? Write them in the chart.

Chapter 1	Chapter 2	Chapter 3

Part Two: God

1. Read Titus chapters one through three.

2. What do you learn about God in each chapter? (Don't worry about noting every detail given. Write the facts that stand out to you and all that you have room for.)

chapter 1	chapter 2	chapter 3

3. Review the chart above. Circle the fact that stands out to you the most. Is there a fact about God that you find challenging to trust? Is there a fact about God that is new to you?

Part Three: Author

1. Read Titus 1-3. Look for general information about the author.

> You are only looking for facts about Paul from this letter, not what you know of him from other letters.

2. List brief facts about the author (i.e., where he is, what he is doing, and why) to get a general idea of who wrote to Titus.

3. What is the author's tone in this letter?

4. What pastoral qualities does the author have that you find to be important? Write a sentence describing the author.

5. Where was Paul when he wrote this letter?

Part Four: Recipients

1. Read Titus again. What is going on with Titus? (Remember your answers should be brief facts from the Titus text. It is okay to re-write the same facts; keep in mind that you only need to write a few facts.)

2. What are the specific, personal instructions to Titus?

3. What do you learn about the Cretans? How are they described? How does Paul describe the reputation of the Cretans?

4. How do you see the Cretans' need for spiritual leadership and order in the church?

5. Do you believe the gospel is powerful enough to bring about change to a "Cretan type" community? How does the gospel penetrate a wayward culture like this?

6. How can a church affect a "Cretan type" community? What is required of the church to influence their community?

7. Define *Crete 2914* to give you a better understanding of this city.

This is your first word study! Please note, if this is new to you, it may seem challenging at first. See "Lost in Translation" at the end of this study.

This becomes easier with practice!

8. Look for information on the internet or in a Bible resource and research the island of Crete. What was Crete known for?

9. How did the Cretans come to know the gospel (see Acts 2:11)?

Part Five: Purpose

1. Read through Titus once more to discover Paul's purpose(s) for writing. Why did Paul write to Titus? List the purpose(s) for the letter.

> Often an author indicates his purpose with words like "for this reason, so that, in order to, for, because, therefore, nevertheless, indeed, so."

2. According to the letter to Titus, what can you determine about God's *church*? How are God's people to worship?

3. Consult a commentary and read only the *introduction* to Titus. (Ask your pastor for a commentary recommendation.) Please do not read further than the introduction as you do not want to spoil your study in the days ahead. Find out when this letter was written and any other background information to aid in a better understanding of the *Survey* of Titus. Some things that you will want to look for in your commentary reading include the following:

    a. The date written.

    b. Look for a map of Crete.

Who was Titus?

In-Class Worksheet

1. What does Paul call Titus in Titus 1:4?

2. Cross-reference the following Scriptures and note what you learn about Titus.

2 Corinthians 2:12-13

2 Corinthians 7:6-7

2 Corinthians 7:13-15

2 Corinthians 8:6

2 Corinthians 8:16

2 Corinthians 8:23

2 Corinthians 12:18

Galatians 2:1-3

3. Describe the relationship between Paul and Titus. How did they establish and cultivate their relationship?

4. How did Paul and Titus model a discipleship relationship?

5. How did Paul and Titus regard the local church? How did they regard the lost?

6. Write a short summary describing Titus.

Rejoice in Lord always; again I will say, rejoice.
Philippians 4:4

Gospel Godliness

Lesson Two: Titus 1:1-9

But you are near, O Lord, and all your commandments are true.
Long have I known from your testimonies that you have founded them forever.

—Psalm 119:151-152

Part One: Chapter Survey

1. Prayerfully read Titus chapter one.

2. Complete the chapter one Survey Worksheet located at the end of this lesson.

3. Under what authority does Paul serve as an Apostle (Titus 1:1-3)?

> Please note, this first chapter Survey may appear to be overwhelming. Be patient! You are organizing the chapter's facts onto a worksheet to help you gather information to better understand the context. You will begin to gain understanding as you work, following the steps prescribed.

4. How does Paul greet Titus (Titus 1:4)?

Part Two: Know and Grow

1. Who is a believer's faith to represent?

2. Read Titus 1:1-3. In one word, state what Paul expects a believer's faith to represent.

3. What does Paul say about *faith*? Read Titus chapter one and color a blue box around the word *faith,* and then list all that Paul says about faith. Also mark *faith* in Titus 2:2, 10.

4. Do all religions have the same faith? What does Paul mean by *faith*? Define *faith 4102.*

5. How does someone come to faith? Read Romans 10:17.

6. For whom is Paul writing? Define *elect 1588.*

> Does this definition cause you concern?

7. How do new Christians begin to become godly in character? What does a woman need to understand before she can obey God's word?

    a. What will lead to godliness (Titus 1:1)?

    b. Define *knowledge 1922.*

8. What does personal knowledge of Christ produce in a believer? Define *godliness 2150.*

9. Read Philippians 1:9-11 and 1 Timothy 2:1-11, 4:6-9. According to these passages, what does godliness look like in the life of a woman?

10. Paul's purpose was to promote believers' spiritual health and growth. Reflect on these personal application questions: Who promotes your faith and helps you grow spiritually? Are you in a Biblical church where you are submitting to sound teaching and accountable to the elders of your church? Do you sense that you are increasing in the knowledge of the truth? Does your life reflect your Godward attitude? Take time to reflect prayerfully on your personal relationship with God.

Part Three: Hope

1. How often do you think about eternal life? Do you trust that you will have eternal life? Or do you at times doubt the certainty of eternal life?

2. Read Titus 1:1-3 and answer the following questions:

   a. What is godliness founded on?

   b. What did God promise?

   c. How did God make known His promise of eternal life?

   d. When?

   e. To whom?

   f. What validates His promise?

3. What if we couldn't trust God to keep His word? How would that influence our hope?

4. What is the hope that Paul has in mind (Titus 1:2)? Define *hope 1680.*

5. Paul has much to say about *hope* in this letter; read through Titus and look for the word *hope*. Mark *hope* with a blue triangle, and then note what you learn. (The word *hope* is used in all three chapters.)

6. Consider the following verses on *hope*. Highlight the word *hope* and note what you learn. How do these verses cause you to focus on heavenly things? May these truths cause you to meditate joyfully on the heavenly life.

Romans 5:5 and hope does not put us to shame, because God's love has been poured into our hearts through the Holy Spirit who has been given to us.

Romans 8:24-25 For in this hope we were saved. Now hope that is seen is not hope. For who hopes for what he sees? But if we hope for what we do not see, we wait for it with patience.

Romans 14:4 Who are you to pass judgment on the servant of another? It is before his own master that he stands or falls. And he will be upheld, for the Lord is able to make him stand.

Romans 15:13 May the God of hope fill you with all joy and peace in believing, so that by the power of the Holy Spirit you may abound in hope.

Colossians 1:4-5 ...[Since]... we heard of your faith in Christ Jesus and of the love that you have for all the saints, because of the hope laid up for you in heaven. Of this you have heard before in the word of truth, the gospel.

Colossians 1:27 To them God chose to make known how great among the Gentiles are the riches of the glory of this mystery, which is Christ in you, the hope of glory.

Hebrews 6:18b-19 ...[Since]... it is impossible for God to lie, we who have fled for refuge might have strong encouragement to hold fast to the hope set before us. We have this as a sure and steadfast anchor of the soul, a hope that enters into the inner place behind the curtain.

Hebrews 10:23 Let us hold fast the confession of our hope without wavering, for he who promised is faithful.

May these truths cause you to joyfully meditate on the heavenly life.

7. How does hope of eternal life urge you toward godly living? How does having hope about our future affect how we live today?

8. How are faith, knowledge, godliness, and hope of eternal life intermingled in the life of a believer?

9. Considering Titus' circumstances, what did Paul want Titus to understand about the God of hope?

10. We have the *hope* of eternal life because of the finished work of Jesus Christ. Think about your own experiences with the gospel. Do you have the hope of eternal life? If you died today, would you be in heaven with Jesus Christ? It is our prayer that you would be made an heir, according to the hope of eternal life. If you do not know if you have this certain hope, please cry out to the Lord and talk with a church leader.

Part Four: Church Leadership

1. Read Titus 1:4-9. Who is in charge of church leadership? Who will build the church? Read Matthew 16:18 and Ephesians 5:23. Is Scripture clear about the authority of the church?

2. List the two things Titus was to do in Crete.

3. Define *set in order 1930* and *elder 4245.*

4. List the elder qualifications (Titus 1:5-9). Define any word that causes you question.

> Based on the elder qualifications, what are the roles and functions of elders?

5. Which qualification is repeated? What is significant about the repetition?

6. Consider these questions and write a response: Are the requirements for appointing church leadership as simple as making a checklist? Are there ever exceptions to these leadership standards? What would happen if these qualifications were compromised? What if the church elders do not meet the qualifications?

7. Paul says more about church leadership to Timothy in 1 Timothy 3:1-7. What are the qualifications for church leadership, according to this passage?

8. *Elder* is one of the titles for a church leader; what is the other title Paul mentions in Titus 1:7? What other titles are synonymous to elder in the New Testament?

Cross-reference Acts 20:28; Ephesians 4:11; and 1 Timothy 3:1. Note their specific role or responsibility as indicated.

9. Is the role of *elder* gender specific?

10. Why are elders significant to the church?

Part Five: Hold Firm

1. Read again Titus 1:1-9. What did Paul have in mind for the Cretan churches, beginning with ordered leadership? What sphere of influence do leaders have (for good or for bad)?

2. What were church leaders expected to do (Titus 1:9)? What is the relationship and responsibility between an elder and the word of God? Define *hold firm 472*.

3. In order for the elder to teach someone the word of God, what does he need to know for himself? Define *sound 5198* and *doctrine 1319*.

4. What would an elder need to know to rebuke someone for contradicting the word of God? Define *rebuke 3870*.

5. Cross reference a few of these scriptures: Acts 6:4; 1 Timothy 3:1-7, 4:6, 14, 5:17; and 2 Timothy 2:2, 15, 24.

6. How do pastors decide what to preach? Paul calls it a *stewardship* in 1 Timothy 1:4. Are there prerequisites to preaching and teaching? See Ezra 7:10, 25; Deuteronomy 31:12– 13; Nehemiah 8:1-9; and Colossians 1:28-29.

7. Why is it important to hold fast the word of God?

   a. When an elder *holds fast* the word, what kind of worshiper is he?

   b. Cross-reference John 4:23. What kind of worshiper was God seeking in Crete?

   c. How do true worshipers influence their neighbors?

   d. Would God seek after you? Are you a true worshiper?

   e. Are all church-goers necessarily true worshipers?

8. What if an elder does not hold firm to the word? What hope do people have if there is no sound doctrine in the church? (Think of the culture of the Cretan churches at the time of Paul's letter.)

9. Read from commentary resources through Titus 1:9. Record notes as needed.

10. How do you better understand Paul's purpose for the letter to Titus?

Sophron Studies

Survey Worksheet

I. What words are repeated in chapter one? List seven to ten words.

II. Read chapter one and mark in red every reference to God (Father, Jesus Christ, Holy Spirit). Fill in the chart with facts about God from this chapter.

> One fact about God can bring about many *attributes* of His character.
> For example:
>
> Fact: God never lies.
> Attributes: God is truth, reliable, faithful.

God the Father	God the Son	God the Holy Spirit	Attributes of God
elects (1:1) *never lies (1:2)*			*Gracious because He elects.* *Honest and trustworthy because He doesn't lie.*

III. What information does Paul tell us about himself? Note every time *Paul* is mentioned and color-code his name and any reference to his name (pronouns) in light blue. Note all that he wanted Titus and the Cretans (and us) to know about him.

IV. Note every time the author says *you* or *your* or any other reference to the recipients (i.e., brothers). Color any reference to Titus and the Cretans in orange. What information does Paul reveal about Titus and the recipients in Crete?

V. Describe the churches in Crete (facts from chapter one only).

VI. What is the main verse that best summarizes this chapter? Title chapter one.

The Church Body

In-Class Worksheet
←———————⟨⟨⟨

Have you wondered why the church is called a body?
Whose body does the church represent?
Who makes up the church body?

1. Cross-reference the following to learn more about the body of Christ:

Matthew 16:18

Acts 2:37-47

Acts 20:28

1 Corinthians 12:27-28

Ephesians 4:15-16

Ephesians 5:23-27

Colossians 1:18

Colossians 1:24-25

1 Timothy 3:15

2. Consider how the elders and the church body live out ministry within the church:

Acts 8:4

Romans 12:3-8

Romans 12:10-13

Romans 15:26

1 Corinthians 5:1-13

2 Thessalonians 3:14

2 Peter 3:1-2

James 1:27

1 Timothy 5:1-4

3. Write out your understanding of the design and function of the church body.

*So then, as we have opportunity, let us do good to everyone,
and especially to those who are of the household of faith.*

Galatians 6:10

Sound Faith

Lesson Three: Titus 1:10-16

Your decrees are very trustworthy;
holiness befits your house, O Lord, forevermore.

—Psalm 81:16

Part One: Unsound Doctrine

1. Read Titus 1:10-16. This passage is about whom?

2. How does Paul describe the false teachers (Titus 1:10-16)?

3. Recall what the elders are to do with false teachers (Titus 1:9).

4. Do our churches today struggle with false teachers?

5. Read each reference below and chart the information in the appropriate column:

   Acts 20:29-32   Romans 16:17-18   2 Corinthians 11:13
   Colossians 2:20-23   1 Timothy 4:1-3   2 Timothy 3:6-7
   2 Peter 2:1-3, 18-19   2 Peter 3:3, 17-18   Jude 8-13

How are the false teachers described?	What do the false teachers do? How?	Why do they teach falsely? What is their motive?	What are the dangers of false teaching?	What are the warnings for the false teachers?

6. Read over the chart. Do these details alarm you? How can false teachers instill fear?

7. What must we know, in order to detect error? What is the church's defense against the false teachers?

8. Why do people in the church follow false teachers? Cross-reference 1 Timothy 4:1 and 2 Timothy 4:3-4.

9. How many false teachers were among the Cretans (Titus 1:10)?

10. Summarize how the false teachers are dangerous to the church.

Part Two: Unashamed

1. Read Titus 1:10-16. How was Titus to deal with false teachers?

2. Why was it urgent for Titus to oppose and silence them? How did the false teachers affect the church members (Titus 1:11)?

3. What were the false teachers doing or not doing within the churches of Crete (Titus 1:10)?

4. What does insubordinate mean? Define *insubordinate 506*.

5. What does empty talk sound like? What value do empty talkers place on the word of God? What value do empty talkers place on eternity?

6. Do you think that Titus would have been jolted into considering "who" among him may have been deceiving him and his fellow believers? What do deceivers look like? Who do they try to imitate?

7. Who are those of the *circumcision party* (Titus 1:10)? Cross-reference Acts 11:2, 15:1, 24 and Galatians 1:13, 2:4, 12, 4:21.

8. What motivated the false teachers in Crete?

9. Practically, how would the elders have applied the word and worship to the "upset" families (Titus 1:11)? What would sound doctrine reveal to a confused congregation? Cross-reference Romans 15:4 and 2 Timothy 3:16-17.

10. Is teaching sound doctrine a problem today? How does today's culture of sound doctrine compare to the time when Titus was in Crete? Whose job is it to ensure the proper teaching of sound doctrine?

Part Three: Rebuking Sin

1. Read Titus 1:12-13. How is the typical Cretan described?

2. Do you know of anyone who could be characterized by these descriptions?

3. How do we know if this description is accurate?

4. Take a few minutes to read commentaries and research the prophet who is noted for describing the Cretans (Titus 1:12).

5. How would a *born again* Cretan be characterized? How would believing Cretans have been challenged by their culture?

6. How did Paul instruct Titus to deal with the false teachers of Crete (Titus 1:13)? Define *rebuke 1651* and *sharply 664*.

7. Why does Paul emphasize the instruction to rebuke in Titus 1:9 and 1:13?

8. Cross-reference Titus 2:15 and 1 Timothy 5:20. What do you learn about the practice of *rebuking*?

9. What is the danger in *not* addressing sin? Read 1 Corinthians 5:6-9.

10. How does rebuking sin and false teachers preserve and promote church order?

Part Four: Sound in the Faith

1. Read Titus 1:13-14. Why was Titus to rebuke the sinful Cretans?

2. What does it mean to be *sound* in the faith? (Recall the definition for *sound* in Lesson 2, Part Five.) What was it that Paul wanted for the Cretan churches?

3. Mark the word *sound* with an arrow and note what you learn from marking *sound* in Titus 1:9, 13, 2:1, 2:2, and 2:8.

   a. How would a *sound* faith change the way that someone thinks and lives?

   b. How would living out a *sound* faith affect the church?

4. If the church leaders of Crete were focused on sound doctrine, to what would they not be devoted (Titus 1:14)?

5. Were Jewish myths important? Did they hold value to the Christians in Crete? Did the myths present a danger to the church? Cross-reference 2 Timothy 4:4.

6. Can you think of a modern-day myth that people in the church community hold on to? Is it ever a good practice to hold on to myths?

7. What were the commandments of men (Titus 1:14)? Whose rules did they wish for the people to follow? What is the danger in man-made commandments? Read Matthew 15:9 and Colossians 2:20-23.

8. What man-made rules are you passionate about? How do churches today present *commandments of men*? What are some issues of legalism? How do you think legalism begins? Where do man-made laws lead (Titus 1:14)?

9. Thank God for your healthy church! Pray to discern if there are any hints of legalism in your own life. Pray to never turn away from truth. Keep in mind that if it wasn't a real threat, Paul would not have included it.

10. Compare *holding fast to the trustworthy word* (Titus 1:9) to *turning away* from the truth (Titus 1:14). What is the believer's safeguard? Are we exempt from the possibility of turning away? How does God see fit to protect His church from false teachers, myths, and the commandments of men?

Part Five: Unbelievers in the Church

1. Read Titus 1:15-16. Who are the pure? Define *pure 2513*.

2. Cross-reference Proverbs 20:9; Matthew 5:8; Acts 10:15; and 2 Timothy 2:22. What do you learn about those who are *pure*?

3. Would you put yourself in the "pure" category, rather than the "defiled" category? How is that possible? Read Titus 3:3-7.

4. What is the opposite of pure? How are those "defiled," described in Titus 1:15-16?

    a. What do the defiled say?

    b. What do the defiled do?

    c. How do those defiled approach the gospel?

5. How does God view the defiled (Titus 1:16)? Cross-reference Ephesians 5:5-6.

6. What do the pure and those defiled have in common?

Personal reflection: Is there anything in your own life that may suggest defilement? How are you surrounding yourself with sound doctrine?

7. How does biblical church order reflect Jesus Christ?

8. Read from commentary resources through Titus 1:16.

9. Summarize Titus chapter one.

10. How does chapter one hold to Paul's purpose of this letter?

Sophron Studies

Pray That They Would be Sound in the Faith

In-Class Activity

When you read Titus 1:16, who comes to mind? Are you discouraged by someone's hypocrisy? Do you feel as though you are "judging" others? Perhaps you live in the Bible belt where cultural Christianity is a way of life. Then again, maybe your parents are still in a denomination that promotes works, discounting the sufficiency of Christ's work on the cross. While realizing close friends and family members may not be genuinely saved is a devastating thought, we have the privilege to pray for their souls.

You can pray...

Pray for family members who are resistant to the gospel; pray they would come to know Christ as Lord.

In general, pray for those closest to you who profess to know God, but deny Him by their deeds. Ask the Lord to draw them to be sound in the faith.

Below are some Scriptures that you can use to pray for others to come to salvation. If there is another passage that you use for salvation prayers, please share it with the group.

Make _____ to know your ways; teach _____ your paths. Lead _____ and teach her (Psalm 25:4).

All the paths of the Lord are steadfast love and faithfulness, for those who keep his covenant and his testimonies (Psalm 25:10). Lord, cause _____ to keep your covenant and testimonies.

The friendship of the Lord is for those who fear him, and he makes known to them his covenant (Psalm 25:14). Lord make _____ to fear you. Would you make your covenant known to him?

Lord, would you open the eyes of _____ so that they may turn from darkness to light and from the power of Satan to God, that _____ may receive forgiveness of sins and a place among those who are sanctified by faith in Jesus Christ (Acts 26:18).

Lord will you deliver _____ from the domain of darkness and transfer her to the kingdom of your beloved Son, in whom we have redemption, the forgiveness of sins (Colossians 1:13-14).

Lord would you cause _____ to put off his old self... and be renewed in the spirit of his mind, and to put on the new self, created after the likeness of God in true righteousness and holiness (Ephesians 4:22-24).

And hope does not put us to shame, because God's love has been poured into our hearts through the Holy Spirit who has been given to us (Romans 5:5). Lord, we know that hope does not put us to shame, will you pour out your love to _____ through your Holy Spirit?

Blessed be the God and Father of our Lord Jesus Christ! According to His great mercy, will you, Lord, cause _____ to be born again to a living hope (1 Peter 1:3)?

Write your own prayer(s) here.

Relationships

Lesson Four: Titus 2:1-3

Entrust to faithful men who will be able to teach others also.

—*2 Timothy 2:2b*

Part One: Chapter Two Survey

1. Read Titus chapter 2.

2. Complete the chapter two Survey Worksheet located at the end of this lesson.

3. How does chapter two connect with chapter one?

4. What is Paul contrasting in Titus 2:1? What does Paul expect of Titus?

Part Two: Older Men

1. Read Titus 2:2. What is expected of older men? Define any of these words that you do not know.

2. Were the older men in the Cretan churches valued and honored, as part of the church's order? Scripture gives wisdom for honoring the aged. Cross-reference Leviticus 19:32; Job 12:12; Psalm 71:18; Proverbs 16:31, 23:22, and 1 Timothy 5:1.

3. What things has an older man learned over the years of being a Christian, according to Titus 2:2? Also cross-reference 2 Timothy 2:22.

4. How does the older man's life testify *to knowledge leading to godliness*? Consider the following questions:

    a. How does the older man contribute to the spiritual health of the church?

    b. How does the older man support the elders within his church?

    c. How does he promote sound doctrine?

    d. How does the older man regard man-made laws?

    e. What do his works tell others about God?

5. How could the older man's love for God and others bring healing to the upset families in Crete? What could the older man's love do for those in the community who are hurting?

6. How do the descriptions for the older men compare to the qualifications of elders? What would be reasons the *older man* would not be suited for church leadership?

7. Are all older men characterized by the description in Titus 2:2? Do all men eventually get to this description?

8. What is our culture's general opinion of the aged?

9. As women, what are we to do with these expectations of the older men? What should be our attitude toward the older men in our church?

10. Take time to bow to the Father; praise God for the older men in your church. Pray that their love and wisdom would increase, their bodies persevere, and that they would bear much fruit in godly living as they hold fast the faithful word.

Part Three: Reverent, Older Women

1. How do you think most people view women *in* the church?

2. Read 1 Timothy 5:1-2. How did Paul instruct Timothy to be in relationship with women in the congregation? What does this tell us about the biblical value of women in the church?

3. Read Titus 2:2-5. What is expected of older women?

4. Note the word "likewise" in Titus 2:3. Why did Paul use the word "likewise?" In what way(s) does the older woman share in the qualifications of the older man?

5. Discuss how this list of godly expectations differs from the way of the world.

6. What comes to mind when you think of a *reverent* woman? Do you aspire to be like her?

7. How do other Bible translations state the *reverent* woman? Read Titus 2:3 in other translations.

8. Define *reverent 2412.* Please note the root meaning of this word.

9. Find the opposite of a *reverent* woman. What is the older woman *not* to be like?

10. How does an irreverent woman affect the church?

Part Four: Old Testament Priests

1. How would you describe an Old Testament priest? Do you think you would have much in common with him?

2. The Apostle Paul compares the older woman's reverent behavior and duty to that of a priest. Consider some of the following passages and complete the chart.

Exodus 19:5-6, 28:1-3, 29:35-46, 40:13-15   Leviticus 10:8-11, 21:21, 23

Numbers 3:38, 6:22-27   Deuteronomy 21:5

1 Chronicles 23:28-32   Ezekiel 22:23-31

1 Peter 2:5, 9   Malachi 1:1-9

Who were the Priests?	Priestly Duties	How did they become a priest?	The outcome of not performing duties

3. Read over the facts in the chart. What stands out to you?

4. Old Testament priests had many duties to perform; how can you relate to their multitasking? How do these priestly duties apply to you?

5. What are some of the parallels for godly women and the Old Testament priests?

6. Have you been appointed a priestess? Would you consider yourself to be a reverent woman? Are you growing in holiness? What convictions come to mind?

7. How does understanding that the woman is to be holy, like a priestess, bring a higher honor and importance to the instruction in Titus 2:3?

Part Five: Still Sacrificing

1. Praise God that we no longer need to sacrifice animals to atone for sin! What are the sacrifices that we are to offer? See Hosea 6:6, Psalm 51:16-17, 116:17, 141:2 and Romans 12:1-2.

2. Could someone other than a priest perform the priestly duties? Also see Numbers 1:50-53 and Exodus 31:7-10, 32:1-10.

3. How would a reverent, "priestly" older woman influence a "Cretan type" community? Read Philippians 2:15-16.

4. Read Proverbs 14:1. How can a godly woman influence others? What two options for influence does a woman have?

5. Where does a godly woman's influence begin?

6. How do you think the women in the Cretan congregation responded to Titus's instructions and expectations?

7. Do the older women that you know aim to be reverent? Are they holding fast to the faithful word and letting the Word produce in them a Godward attitude? How can you tell if they are becoming holy?

8. If you had a spiritual mother (as one compared to a priest), what did she model for you and others?

9. Will you take time now to write a thank you note to a woman who models the biblical expectation of a reverent woman, a priestess? Consider telling her how you have been encouraged by her influence and her personal pursuit of holiness.

10. Spend time in prayer for the godly women around you. This would serve them well! The reverent women in your church would appreciate your intercessory prayer. Ask our Father to help them remain faithful, to abound in love, and to never grow weary in doing good.

Sophron Studies ←←←

Survey Worksheet

I. What words and themes are repeated in Titus chapter two?

II. Read chapter two and mark in red every reference to God (Father, Jesus Christ, Holy Spirit). Fill in the chart with facts about God from this chapter.

God the Father	God the Son Jesus Christ	God the Holy Spirit	Attributes of God

III. What information does Paul tell us about himself in chapter two? Note every time *Paul* is mentioned and color-code his name and any reference to his name (pronouns) in light blue. What did Paul want Titus and the Cretans (and us) to know about him?

IV. Does Paul reveal any new information about Titus? What do you learn about the Cretans?

V. Complete the chart to organize the facts of the various roles expected for church order (Titus chapter two).

Who	Instructions for an Orderly Body
Older men	
Young men	
Older women	
Younger women	
Slaves	
Titus	

VI. Which verse best summarizes this chapter? Title this chapter.

Teaching and Training

Lesson Five: Titus 2:3-5

She opens her mouth in wisdom,
and the teaching of kindness is on her tongue.

—Proverbs 31:26

Part One: She Says

1. Read Titus 2:3-5. List the characteristics of a woman's reverent behavior in the appropriate column in the chart below.

What she is to do:	*What she is not to do:*

2. Summarize the older woman's responsibilities.

3. How is a reverent woman to speak? How is she *not* to speak? Cross-reference a few of the following passages: Titus 2:5; Proverbs 10:19-20, 31-32, 12:18, 25:15, 31:26; 2 Corinthians 12:20; Ephesians 4:31; Colossians 3:8, 4:6; and James 3:1-12.

4. What is the woman of God capable of doing with her tongue (Titus 2:3)? What is a *slanderer 1228*?

5. According to James 3:13-18, what is at the heart of our words? What does James say is the fuel for our tongue?

6. What can our tongues tell others about God?

7. How do reverent women train their tongues?

8. Read Titus 2:3. The reverent woman is not to be enslaved; define *enslaved 1402*.

9. Do you think enslavement to wine would have been an issue in the Cretan culture?

10. How would a woman enslaved to wine have conflict with her *priestly* duties?

Part Two: She Teaches

1. How are older women to be in relationship with younger women?

2. What is the woman of God to teach others? What might that include?

3. Define the original meaning of the phrase *teaching what is good 2567*.

4. How does the older woman practically teach good things? How does the older woman *provide superior benefit* to the younger woman? Do you think that this applies to all women in some fashion – to either be instructing someone or be taught by someone?

5. Consider Romans 12:1-2. How does the older woman promote godly living?

6. In the context of the local church, who is the older woman to teach (Titus 2:3-4)? How easy is it to build these relationships? What should be the biblical pattern of teaching and training (Titus 2:4 and 2 Timothy 2:1-2)?

7. Prayerfully consider the following questions:

   a. Do you have questions about your role in the church, your church?

   b. What is at stake if the younger women are not trained?

   c. What are possible consequences for the older woman who neglects to fulfill her role?

8. What if an older woman hesitates and / or refuses to invest in a younger woman? What if a younger woman is too busy or does not see the value in having a spiritual mother in her life? What are common excuses from both older and younger women who avoid discipleship relationships?

9. How does the older woman investing in the younger woman affect the church? How serious is this Titus 2:3-5 mandate?

10. Take some time to read again Titus chapters one through three. How do you see the woman's role fitting in with Paul's purpose of this letter?

Part Three: She Models

1. Scripture is exemplary in showing us many holy women who serve as older women modeling reverence. Think of women in the Bible who taught other women, who lived a life of personal holiness, and were sound in their faith. Who comes to mind?

2. Read the example of a reverent woman in Proverbs 31:10-31. What are your thoughts about this woman?

3. Do you think that an average church-going woman can be like the Proverbs 31 woman?

4. How does the Proverbs 31 woman display a reverent behavior? How did the Proverbs 31 woman demonstrate that her life was dedicated to God?

5. Reflect on the reverent woman (Titus 2:3-5) and the excellent woman (Proverbs 31). Consider how an older, *reverent and excellent,* Cretan woman would counsel a *confused and upset* younger woman.

6. Read the account of a special relationship in Luke 1:26-45. What do you think Elizabeth (the older woman) had done in previous years to mentor the younger woman? Why did the younger woman go to Elizabeth?

7. How do you see Elizabeth (Luke 1:26-45) implementing the Titus 2:3-5 mandate?

8. How can a woman influence her family, her church, and her community?

9. Consider the women that Paul rebuked in Philippians 4:2-3. Describe their influence on the church. What was to be done about their issue?

   a. How could a woman's personal sin affect an entire church?

   b. Is the older woman's life always an example?

10. Will you take a few minutes to pray for your women's ministry? Pray for those in charge of Bible study, women in the mission field, and the stay-at-home volunteers. Pray that godly women would be sound in doctrine, sound in their own thinking, and sound in the way they live in their own homes.

Part Four: She Initiates

1. Where do you find confidence to be a godly woman? Do you have cause to boast in what the Lord has done to make you a holy woman? What Scripture do you run to, to remember how you can be a confident woman? Read Proverbs 3:26 and Psalm 20:7-8.

2. Do you think the older women in Crete hesitated to train younger women? Did they ever question their value (their God-given value)?

3. How do you see more clearly your need for Jesus Christ to enable you to be a godly, obedient, reverent woman?

4. Are you one who displays the characteristics of the "Titus 2" woman? How can you encourage women to understand their importance of being reverent women in the body of Christ?

5. Think of your own church congregation; with whom can you share your life? Who will you purpose to train? Will you be intentional in living out Titus 2:3-5 in your local church?

Who are you teaching? Who is teaching you?

6. Will you check to see what is upcoming on your church's calendar that you can invite an older or younger woman to? Will you initiate the invitation? What is it that would draw an older woman to want to take an interest in a younger woman's life or vice versa? Hint: the answer is very simple!

7. Will you make an effort right now to visit with an older or younger woman today? Does that seem risky? Would it be out of your comfort zone? Will you call, email, or text a woman and schedule time with her to purpose to get to know her? You never know, she just may need some special encouragement today.

8. What is another practical way that you can interact with someone who is not in your generation?

9. Think of something that you wish you would have known 25 years ago. Is there a younger woman in your life with whom you can share this?

10. Think about your next 25 years, and imagine the gospel stories that will be written on your own heart. Is there an older woman you can talk to?

Part Five: She is Purposeful

1. Read Titus 2:2-5. Complete the following chart with specifics from the text.

What is the older woman to model, teach and train the younger woman to do? (Titus 2:2-5)	What is the younger woman to learn from the older woman's example and instruction? (Titus 2:3-5)

2. How does the older woman teach character development, life skills, and genuine submission?

3. Where do younger women have the most opportunity to practice all that they are learning?

4. Why are younger women to learn the ways of godly older women (Titus 2:5)?

5. What is the opposite of *revile* according to Titus 2:9-10?

6. Read 2 Timothy 4:10-21. Who was known for doing good works? Who was known for their bad works? Are you known in your church? What is it about *you* that would cause your pastor to name your name to others?

7. Read Philippians 1:27 and answer the following questions:

   a. What is Paul's instruction?

   b. How is this to be done?

   c. Practically, where is this lived out?

   d. Why?

8. In one sentence, summarize what the older woman is to teach and train the younger woman to do.

9. How is the Lord prompting you to respond to these truths?

    a. If you are a younger woman, do you desire to be wisely trained by an older woman who is walking the walk she talks? If you are not being trained, pray for the Lord to bring an older woman into your life to offer you the *schooling* you need to help you with sound doctrine, sound thinking, and sound living.

    b. Perhaps you are an older woman with experiences bursting from your core--- are you seeking younger women to teach and train? How are you urged to share your life? If you are not training a younger woman, please pray and ask the Lord to bring that special young woman to you so that you can train her and enjoy life even more as you reflect on life lessons within the gift of the local church. Will you train a younger woman?

10. Will you help your sister in Christ stand firm and walk in a manner worthy of the gospel? How does the hope of eternal life give you the courage to act in obedience, despite any fears or reservations that you may harbor?

Teach to Think

Lesson Six: Titus 2:4-5

Let the wise hear and increase in learning,
and the one who understands obtain guidance

—Proverbs 1:5

Part One: Biblical Thinking

1. What was the first instruction for Titus (Titus 1:5)?

   a. Who is to lead the church?

   b. What was (is) to fuel the elders to lead the church?

   c. How did Paul intend for the older women to know how to train the younger women?

   d. How did Paul intend for the younger women in the church to be trained?

   e. Do you see the pattern for an ordered church?

2. Cross-reference 1 Timothy 4:7-8; 2 Timothy 3:16-17; and Hebrews 4:12; and then note what you learn about the word of God. Can we be trained in godliness without the word of God?

3. Are you capable of controlling the thoughts that enter your mind?

4. Read Titus 2:2-5. How does the older woman represent sound doctrine (the context of Titus)? What is the relationship of sound doctrine and sound living for the older women of Crete?

5. Read Titus 2:4 in other bible translations. According to this verse, what is the older woman to teach and train the younger woman to do?

6. Women are to be sober and self-controlled biblical thinkers; define *sober 4994*.

    a. How is self-control lived out? How are believers able to achieve this control? Read Titus 2:11-14 and Galatians 5:22-25.

    b. In what areas of life is it more difficult to be self-controlled? How can the culture take its toll on the church in the area of self-control or a lack of self-control?

    c. Do you pray for self-control? In what area can you ask the Lord's help?

7. Paul uses this type of self-controlled thinking multiple times in the book of Titus. See Titus 1:8, 2:2, 2:5, 2:6, 2:12 and mark the word(s) for *self-control* with a pink highlighter. List all the facts that you learn from marking *self-control*.

> Is there anyone not expected to have self-control?

8. The New Testament has much to say about right, *sophron* thinking. Cross-reference the following verses. How do these verses help you understand your responsibility to think with self-control, to think biblically?

Mark 5:15

Acts 26:25

Romans 12:3

1 Corinthians 14:20

1 Timothy 2:9, 15

1 Timothy 3:2

2 Timothy 1:7

1 Peter 4:7

9. Based on all you have learned about biblical thinking, how is the older woman to train the younger woman toward right thinking?

10. How can the word of God help you to think with self-control? How does the biblical expectation of *sophron* thinking urge you to study the word of God for yourself?

Will you choose one of the verses from your study time today to claim as your "go-to" verse to help you think rightly, when you don't want to?

Part Two: Love

1. Read Titus 2:4-5. What comes to mind when you think of how someone might teach another how to love? Doesn't loving one's family come naturally? Is it not instinctive?

2. How are the older women to *train* the younger women to love? Define *train 4994*.

3. Why does a woman's mind need to be trained to love her family?

4. What is significant about a wife loving her husband? Define *love husband 5362*.

5. What are practical examples of the older woman training the younger woman to love her husband?

   a. If you are a young woman, what would you like to learn about loving your husband (or your future husband)?

   b. If you are an older woman, what do you wish someone had talked to you about in regards to loving your husband when you were younger?

6. Read 1 Corinthians 13:1-13. How can women love the way Christ intends?

   > Who perfectly reflects these qualities of love?
   >
   >

7. The older women are also to teach the younger women to love their children. Define *love children 5388.*

8. How does the older woman train the younger woman to love her children?

   a. When it comes to loving one's family, what does a sophron woman think about?

   b. What does a sophron woman *not* think about? What are thoughts she should *not* consider? Why is this important to set straight in our minds?

   c. What circumstances may cause a woman to question her love for her family? How does she counter that with *sophron* thinking?

   d. How can an older woman encourage a younger woman to cultivate a loving relationship with a difficult child in the home?

9. How does a woman loving her family relate to order in the church?

10. What are some ways that you have learned to set your mind on a self-controlled, well-governed path?

Part Three: More to Teach

1. Read Titus 2:5. What does a "priestess" teach? Complete the following chart.

Teach her how to be: (Define the Greek word)	How do other Scripture references support this?	Application questions:
Define *self-control 4998*	1 Peter 5:8, 2 Tim 1:7, Titus 2:12	Describe a self-controlled and sensible woman. How does a self-controlled woman prioritize?
Define *pure 53*	1 Peter 1:16, Col 3:8-18, Eph 5:3	Where does modesty begin? How would Titus 1:1 encourage someone towards purity? What feeds into impurity? What are practical ways that you discipline yourself in purity?
Define *worker at home 3626*	1 Timothy 5:13-15 What does Scripture say about working women?	How important is the duty of home-making? What do household chores teach?
Define *kind 18*	Ephesians 4:32, Col 3:12-13	How is kindness taught? How would a *kind* Cretan woman look different than those around her?

2. Read over the facts in the chart. What are your impressions of all that the older woman must teach the younger woman?

Part Four: Submission

1. What is the final characteristic that the older woman is to teach and train the younger woman to do (Titus 2:5)?

2. What thoughts come to mind regarding submission? Is submission an action or attitude?

3. Define *submission 5293*. How have you seen submission throughout the letter to Titus?

4. Read Ephesians 5:21-33 and answer the following questions:

   a. Who is to be submissive?

   b. What does marriage represent?

   c. Who is glorified in a godly marriage?

   d. What must the wife do to be a godly wife?

   e. Define *respect 5399*.

   f. What are the expectations of a godly husband?

5. Think about the first union of marriage; read Genesis 2:18-25. What was and is a woman's first priority and purpose in her marriage? Define *helper 5828*.

6. How are women to take their role of helper to the church body? How do you view the role of helper in the church? How does a woman's created role affect church ministry and influence other relationships?

> Could you imagine life without the Helper? It is unthinkable, isn't it? While we are far from the standard of the Holy Spirit, the principle is the same in that women are vital in their role as helper. Will you prayerfully consider areas in which you need to embrace your helper role? Is there is need for repentance? Spend time with the Lord and confess your resistance to helping, either your own husband or the men in your life or the men at church, etc.
> Enjoy this time of worship between you and your Helper.

7. Scripture offers more encouragement toward submission in marriage; cross-reference 1 Corinthians 7:1-5 and 1 Timothy 2:9-14.

8. What does an unsubmissive woman look like? How is an unsubmissive woman a threat to the order of the church?

9. What is a godly woman to do when her husband is ungodly? Consider 1 Peter 3:1-6.

10. Why is it important that a godly woman order herself under her husband and fulfill her biblical role to love, submit, respect, and help?

Part Five: Reflections

1. Recall Paul's purposes for writing the letter to Titus.

2. What is the purpose for a woman to show love, self-control, be pure, work at home, show kindness and submission (Titus 2:5b)? Define *reviled 987.*

3. How do you represent the word of God? Do you think that you could ever revile God's word? Are there changes that you need to make or perhaps an attitude to tweak, so that you more accurately represent Jesus Christ and His word?

4. What have you learned about biblical relationships within God's church?

5. Describe how the Titus 2:3-5 mandate was designed to help promote order within the church.

6. Does it matter what women do and how we do it? Does it matter what we do in our own homes, when no one is watching? Does it matter how we love, submit, and respect our husbands?

7. Have these truths made you more appreciative of the godly, older women around you? What are your impressions of the older women now?

8. Read from commentary resources through Titus 2:5.

9. Summarize Titus 2:3-5.

10. What are your questions concerning the biblical expectations of women? What has been the most profound truth you have learned in Titus 2:3-5?

Sophron Studies

A Bad Example

1. Scripture warns about women who do not bring glory to God. Read Proverbs 7.

2. Describe the woman of Proverbs 7.

3. What are your personal reflections about the Proverbs 7 woman?

4. What kind of woman reviles God's word without shame?

5. How does the Proverbs 7 woman compare to the reverent woman of Titus 2:3-5 and the excellent woman of Proverbs 31?

6. Do you have a responsibility toward a Proverbs 7 type of woman?

7. What do you know to be true of God's grace (see Titus 2:11-14 and 3:3-7)?

8. Do you feel safe and secure in thinking that you could never become the Proverbs 7 woman?

Gospel Training

Lesson Seven: Titus 2:6-15

Let your adorning be the hidden person of the heart with the imperishable beauty of a gentle and quiet spirit, which in God's sight is very precious.

—1 Peter 3:4

Part One: Young Men

1. What do you think young men may be lacking (generally speaking)?

    a. Are most young men serious about life?

    b. Do most young men tend to act with wisdom?

2. Read Titus 2:6. What is Paul's instruction to Titus? Define *urge 3870*.

3. Review the definition for *self-control 4993*.

    a. How important is self-control in the life of a Christian?

    b. Is the self-control for a younger man different than that expected of others?

4. Scripture gives much warning and recall for younger men. There is a specific warning in Proverbs 7. Skim this Proverb and note upon whom the aggressive woman was preying upon? Why?

5. Do you think there is adequate instruction and appropriate expectation of our younger men today? Do the young men *in* the church act differently than the young men *outside* the church?

6. Who should teach the young men, according to 2 Timothy 2:2? Who was teaching the young men in Crete?

7. What should the young men be taught? One suggestion is found in 1 Timothy 4:7-15. Is there an applicable Scripture passage that comes to your mind?

8. Read Titus 2:7-8, 15. What was also expected of Pastor Titus?

   a. How do these expectations compare to Titus 1:6-9?

   b. Why was Titus to be careful with his words?

   c. Who were his opponents?

   d. Why does it matter what our opponents think of us?

9. To whom are pastors accountable? Read 1 Peter 5:1-9. How does Peter explain a pastor's role? How important is the pastor's role in preserving truth and order?

   a. To whom was Titus accountable?

   b. How was Titus to give honor to the word of God (Titus 2:7-8)?

10. With all that you have studied about men's roles, list the commonalities of men's responsibilities (elders, older men, and younger men) within the church.

If the men around you are not living out the biblical mandate for men, what is the women's role regarding teaching the younger men?

Part Two: Bond-Slaves

1. Read Titus 2:9-10. Who is addressed in these verses? List the instructions to them.

2. Recall again the definition of submission.

3. Why was a slave to be submissive to a master? Read Ephesians 5:21. How does submission affect a congregation? How is an unsubmissive attitude harmful to the church?

4. Research the practice of slavery during the time of Paul's writing this letter. How did this type of slavery differ from the slavery of the Transatlantic Slave Trade?

5. Why would it have been significant for born-again bondservants to be well-pleasing, not argumentative, and showing all good faith? What should have been the reputation of a bondservant in the Cretan church?

6. What instructions are given to the slaves? Cross-reference Colossians 3:17, 22-24; Ephesians 6:5-9; and 1 Timothy 6:1-7.

7. Why are we, as women, to be placing ourselves under the authority of our master (boss), husband, pastors and elders, according to Titus 2:10?

8. Define *adorn 2885*. How does *adorn* relate to *putting things in order* (Titus 1:5)?

9. How can an employee obey Titus 2:9-10 in today's workplace? Are you well-pleasing to your boss (or perhaps others in authority over you)? Is your reputation that of showing all good faith? Can there ever be any exceptions to adorning the doctrine of God our Savior?

10. With all that you have learned, describe how the reverent woman should *adorn* the gospel.

Part Three: Training by Grace

1. Why are we to live reverently, adorning the gospel? (Hint: see Titus 2:9-10 for the reason.)

2. Read Titus 2:11-14. What does Paul teach about salvation and sanctification? Complete the chart below.

Salvation Titus 2:11, 14	*Sanctification* Titus 2:12-13
The grace of God appeared bringing salvation. Jesus Christ gave Himself for us: From what were you and I saved? Read Titus 3:3. How does God save? Read Titus 3:4-7.	We are being trained to: We are being trained to: We are waiting:

3. Consider the chart above:

   a. Highlight in yellow what is to come in the future.

   b. Highlight in orange what Christians are to be doing now.

   c. Highlight in blue what happened in the past.

   d. What does this passage reveal to us about God (past, present, and future)?

4. How do Christians know how to be godly (Titus 2:12)? Define *trains 3811*.

5. What has God provided as our training manual (Titus 1:1)? Do you sense the importance of having sound doctrine (Titus 2:1)?

6. What becomes of a believer's sinful desires? Define *renounce 720*.

7. What is ungodliness and how do we renounce it? Read 1 John 2:15-17. What are examples of worldly passions?

8. What does Paul want the Cretans to understand about godliness and ungodliness?

9. How is sound doctrine and God's grace training you? Consider your own sanctification--- how do you see yourself changing, becoming reverent, becoming more self-controlled, upright, and godly?

10. How are believers to live while awaiting Christ's second appearing? Read Titus 1:1, 2:3-5, 9-14, 3:1-2, 14; and Philippians 2:12-16, 3:12-16. What other verses come to mind?

What does your *waiting* look like?
What are we to be doing between Christ's appearances?

Part Four: A People for His Own Possession

1. Read Titus 2:14. What did Jesus Christ do for His people? Define *redeem 3084* and *purify 2511.*

2. How does this help you understand Christ's saving work? How does this urge you toward holy living, setting your own life in a God-honoring order?

3. For whom did Christ purify for Himself (Titus 2:14)? Define *possession 4041.*

4. Scripture has more encouragement for God's people. Cross-reference:

Exodus 6:7

Exodus 19:5-6

Deuteronomy 7:6

Deuteronomy 26:18-19

1 Peter 2:9-10

5. Do you belong to God? How do these truths reveal God's love for you? How does knowing that you are God's treasured possession fuel your hope and commitment to being a woman who is a helper to her husband, family, church, and culture?

6. What responsibilities are expected of God's special people (Titus 2:14)? Define *zealous 2207.*

7. What do good works say about God's people? What good work do you zealously seek to do?

8. What four things does Paul want Titus to do as a result of Christ's appearing (Titus 2:15)?

9. What were Paul's concerns for Titus (Titus 2:15)?

   a. What was he to declare?

   b. To whom was Titus to declare these things?

   c. How was he to declare these things?

   d. What is the difference between exhorting and rebuking?

   e. Why? What is at stake if Titus did not declare truth?

10. In conclusion, what are some things you will do as a Christian, because of Christ's appearing?

Part Five: Effects of the Gospel

1. How do you think the Cretan church responded to Titus's exhortations? What are the possible reactions and responses from the Cretan congregants as Titus presented these exhortations to the church?

2. How do wise people respond to correction? Read Proverbs 9:8-10.

3. Is your servanthood to the Lord beautiful and attractive? Does your life display a healthy view of God's character or does it distort the reputation of God? Why is it important for the household of God, the church, to be healthy-minded and orderly? Ask God to aid you in becoming a woman who is orderly, one who adorns the gospel.

4. How is the church today to respond to a Cretan-type culture?

5. What does our culture need from you? How can your witness affect those around you?

6. Read Galatians 5:16-24. What fruit would result from living out the gospel, as Paul instructed the Cretans? What would their flesh no longer seek to do?

7. What would have become of the Cretan false teachers when genuine believers lived out the gospel? What would happen to the false teachers' followers, their gain, their man-made laws?

8. What would an outsider looking in at the Cretan church see as the gospel transformed individual lives?

9. Read from commentary resources through Titus 2:15. Remember that commentaries are useful to confirm what we have already studied for ourselves. Often a commentator has done extensive research and can corroborate even extra-biblical information with biblical information---which is helpful for us! Commentaries are always read after inductively studying truth for ourselves.

10. Summarize Titus 2:1-15.

Holy Living

Lesson Eight: Titus 3:1-7

*For what can be known about God is plain to them,
because God has shown it to them.*

—Romans 1:19

Part One: Chapter Survey

1. Read Titus chapter three.

2. Complete the chapter three Survey Worksheet located at the end of the lesson.

3. How does chapter three complement or explain Paul's purposes for writing to Titus?

4. What does Titus chapter three teach about church order?

5. What does Titus chapter three teach about godly living?

Part Two: A Godly Reputation

1. How do you remember to do what you are supposed to do? Do you set reminder alerts on your phone calendar or perhaps you use the old-fashioned sticky notes and have them scattered on your refrigerator door? What are you prone to forget?

2. Read Titus 3:1-2. What was Titus to remind the Cretans?

3. Recall what was going on in the Cretan church. What do you think their governing officials were like?

4. What makes Titus 3:1-2 challenging to practice? Do you think that you have a general attitude of submission? Prayerfully consider your areas of concern in trusting authorities.

5. Do your "feelings" of trust towards your governing officials determine whether you submit to them? Cross-reference Proverbs 21:1.

6. Consider this list of reminders in Titus 3:1-2 and examine your own behaviors. How do you *remember* to do these things? Do you reflect obedience and *sophron* thinking, remembering and obeying?

7. How does a submissive attitude and action show that we are trusting in God?

8. What should be a believer's attitude and responsibility to government authorities (Titus 3:1)? Cross-reference the following verses and note what Scripture teaches us regarding our attitude toward those in authority over us.

Psalm 2:1-4

John 19:10-11

Romans 13:1-8

Ephesians 4:1-2

Colossians 3:12-13

1 Timothy 2:1-3

1 Peter 2:13–17

9. Paul has mentioned submission three times in this letter. What have you learned from his instructions on *submission*? Who is to submit? Also recall Ephesians 5:21.

10. Think of the contrast in the Cretan community between a Christian and a typical Cretan. What would have been obvious about a Christian's lifestyle?

Spend time praying for your government officials.

Part Three: Good Works Adorn

1. What does the world expect from a Christian?

2. What does a Christian's actions and works reveal about her? Read Titus 1:16 to help you answer.

3. What does Paul say about a believer's *good works*? Note what Paul says about *good works* in Titus 1:16, 2:7, 14, 3:1, 5, 8, 14, and draw a purple square around *good works*. List what you learn from marking *good works*.

4. What is the last expectation in the grouping of Titus 3:1-2? Do you think Paul has high expectations of the Cretan believers? Define *courtesy 4240*

5. Paul expected the Cretan believers to show perfect courtesy toward all people. What about those who were outright blasphemous and rebelled against God's word (Titus 3:2)? How were the Cretans in the church to respond?

6. How do you show perfect courtesy toward all people?

7. Why is a good reputation important for believers? Also read Titus 2:7-8.

8. Read Titus 3:3-7. Describe the Cretans prior to their salvation.

9. How would the Cretans have responded to someone showing them perfect courtesy when they were in the midst of their own foolishness, lying, being evil, disobedient, and living ungodly lifestyles?

10. How many believers were in your life prior to your salvation? Were the believers you knew courteous or critical to you in your unsaved state? How can you have compassion and mercy toward those who are unsaved?

Part Four: But He Saved Us

1. What were the Cretans doing when Christ saved them? Were they looking for salvation through the blood of Jesus Christ? Were they cleaning up their acts, to earn God's favor? Do you think that some of the lying, lazy, gluttonous Cretans woke up one day and suddenly decided to be righteous?

2. How did you clean up your life to become right with God? What convinced you of your foolishness, disobedience, straying, hatred and enslavement to worldliness?

3. List all that God did for your salvation (3:4-7). Look up any words that are unfamiliar.

4. Consider your answer in number three (above) and highlight everything you did to earn your salvation.

5. What were the Cretans like when God's goodness and loving kindness appeared to them?

6. What does it mean that God saved us? Define *saved 4982*.

7. Consider Titus 3:4-7; Romans 5:6-10; and Ephesians 2:1-13 and describe the Savior who saves.

8. Consider Paul's gospel presentation in Titus 3:4-7. How does this compare to the letter's introduction in Titus 1:1-2?

9. How does this spur you on to hope, to think of eternity with Jesus Christ, to wait eagerly for His appearing?

10. What is your evangelical approach to share the gospel of Jesus Christ? What do you say? Who do you share Christ with? Will you share the good news with someone this week? Perhaps even invite them to join you in Bible study.

Part Five: Regenerated and Renewed

1. How does salvation work? Why is a spiritual transformation so mysterious?

2. Read Titus 3:4-7. How does Paul detail God's work of salvation?

3. Who is salvation about? Why does God save us (Titus 3:5-7)?

4. What does it mean that God saved us by the washing of regeneration (Titus 3:5)? Define *washing 3067* and *regeneration 3824*.

5. Read the following cross-references and highlight what you learn about God's cleansing.

Ezekiel 36:25-29 I will sprinkle clean water on you, and you shall be clean from all your uncleannesses, and from all your idols I will cleanse you. And I will give you a new heart, and a new spirit I will put within you. And I will remove the heart of stone from your flesh and give you a heart of flesh. And I will put my Spirit within you, and cause you to walk in my statutes and be careful to obey my rules. You shall dwell in the land that I gave to your fathers, and you shall be my people, and I will be your God. And I will deliver you from all your uncleannesses.

1 Corinthians 6:11 And such were some of you. But you were washed, you were sanctified, you were justified in the name of the Lord Jesus Christ and by the Spirit of our God.

Ephesians 5:26 That he might sanctify her, having cleansed her by the washing of water with the word.

Hebrews 10:22 Let us draw near with a true heart in full assurance of faith, with our hearts sprinkled clean from an evil conscience and our bodies washed with pure water.

6. Read John 3:1-17. What must happen for one to be saved? How does this parallel with truth in Titus 3:5?

7. What is the Holy Spirit's role in salvation (Titus 3:5 and John 3:5)? Define *renewal 342* and then cross-reference Romans 12:2.

> What does a renewed mind enable someone to think about?

8. Why is it important to understand the importance of sound doctrine? Can the gospel be the gospel without accuracy?

When did God first make Himself known to you?
How did God save you?

9. Read from commentary resources through Titus 3:7.

10. Summarize Titus 3:1-7.

Survey Worksheet

I. What does Paul emphasize in chapter three? List the repeated words.

II. Read chapter three and mark in red every reference to God (Father, Son, and Holy Spirit). Fill in the chart with facts about God from this chapter.

God the Father	God the Son Jesus Christ	God the Holy Spirit	Attributes of God God is...
goodness and lovingkindness appeared (3:4)		renews	Good Loving and kind Visible

III. What information does Paul tell us about himself in chapter three? Note every time *Paul* is mentioned and color-code his name and any reference to his name in light blue. Record the information below.

IV. What does Paul tell us about Titus? Color any reference to *Titus* in orange. List any information below about Titus from chapter three.

V. What do you learn about the Cretans from chapter three?

VI. What specific instructions are given to Titus in chapter three?

VII. What verse best summarizes this chapter? Title the chapter.

Give Yourself Away

In-Class Worksheet
←———————————⟨⟨⟨

Consider all that you have learned about discipleship relationships as well as what
Paul urges the Christian Cretans to remember in Titus chapter three.
An ordered life invests in others and adheres to the church body.
Consider this worksheet for more encouragement in becoming
Christ-like, in regards to loving others well, loving them sacrificially.

---

1. Read the following cross-references.

Matthew 16:24

Mark 10:45

Philippians 2:5-8

Romans 12:1

Romans 15:1-3

1 Corinthians 6:19-20

1 Corinthians 10:33

1 John 3:16-17

2. How can you ensure a joy-filled attitude as you aspire to do good works? How does this adorn the doctrine of God?

3. Who are the happiest, most joyful, and most content people you know? How do joyful people stay joyful? What might make a miserable person so miserable?

4. Consider your area of service, your attitude in serving, and your actual service toward God's people, how can you maintain joy in doing good works?

5. Is it ever okay to take a little "me" time?

6. How can you be ready for every good work (Titus 3:1)?

7. How do discipleship relationships require you to "give yourself away?" Is the cost worth it?

8. What are some of the blessings from investing in others and serving the body?

May we be women who are zealous for good works,
looking to Jesus as our example in
loving and serving sacrificially.

Doctrine and Duty

Lesson Nine: Titus 3:8-15

Let your adorning be the hidden person of the heart with the imperishable beauty of a gentle and quiet spirit, which in God's sight is very precious.

—1 Peter 3:4

Part One: Devoted to Duty

1. Read Titus 3:1-8. What is the *trustworthy statement*? Why did the Cretans need to be reminded of this statement? (Hint: look back to what Paul just wrote.)

2. What was Titus to insist? Define *insist 1226*.

3. Recall what Titus was to declare in Titus 2:15. What is the commonality in "insisting on these things" and "declaring these things"?

   a. What is it that Paul wants to emphasize to Titus?

   b. What is Titus to emphasize to the church?

   c. How was Titus to emphasize, insist, and declare these things (Titus 2:15)?

4. What are Christians to understand about the gospel? How does the gospel work for those already saved (Titus 1:1, 2:11-14, 3:4-7)?

5. Why was Titus to insist on Titus 3:3-7? What is the expectation of believers?

6. What do you learn about *good works* in Titus 1:16, 2:7, 14, 3:1, 5, 8, 14?

   a. What is Paul's conclusion about good works in Titus 3:8b?

   b. Define *excellent 2570* and *profitable 5624*.

7. As a disciple of Jesus Christ, what are *good works* for women to be devoted to? What do you understand about good works and your obedience? Highlight the following "works" in the word-bank below if you think they are to be considered *good works*:

volunteering in Sunday School	taking a meal to someone who is sick
loving your husband	being faithful to your family
submitting to husband / authorities	spiritual disciplines
encouraging a sister in the Lord	helping someone move
saying "thank you"	training in godliness
renouncing worldly passions	agreeing to a discipleship relationship
going to church	quarreling
devoted to pleasures of the world	standing against the President
memorizing Scripture	working a 9-5 job

*Do you understand that good works are simply doing
what we have been called to do?
An obedient life is a good work!*

8. Cross-reference Ephesians 2:8-10; Colossians 3:23-24; 2 Timothy 2:21; and James 2:14-26. What do you learn about good works?

9. What is the importance of a believer being responsible to do good works?

10. Read James 1:22-27. What is true religion? What does James say about one's response to the word of God? What does he say about works and faith?

Part Two: Be a Peacemaker

1. Read Titus 3:9-11. What and *who* are to be avoided? Why?

2. Have you ever had anything good come from foolish controversies, genealogies, dissensions, and quarrels about the law? Contrast what the godly woman is to say and be known for.

3. Consider the Cretan congregations as they were affected by those described in Titus 3:9-11; what did their church look like? How were the false teachers affecting members (Titus 1:11, 13-14)?

4. How would a church suffer if the leadership did not biblically steward their responsibilities for church order?

5. What are modern-day foolish controversies, genealogies, dissensions, and quarrels about the law? Who is the focus of these discussions? Do they *remember* obedience and submission? Are they insisting on the gospel?

6. How was Titus to handle divisive people (Titus 3:10-11)? Define *warn 3559*.

7. Does this type of church discipline seem unloving? What is Paul's conclusion about the divisive man (Titus 3:11)?

8. What does church discipline promote? Cross-reference Matthew 18:7-20; Romans 16:17-18; and 2 John 9-11.

9. Cross-reference Ephesians 4:1-6. What do you learn about church unity? How dangerous are divisive people to God's church?

10. How is a divisive person harmful to the body of Christ? Why is church unity essential to church order? Is church discipline a good work?

Part Three: Farewell Remarks

1. Read Titus 3:12-15. What are Paul's final words to Titus?

2. What is the only fact we know about Artemas (Titus 3:12)?

3. Who was Tychicus? What is known of him, according to the letter to Titus? Cross-reference Acts 20:4; Ephesians 6:21; Colossians 4:7; and 2 Timothy 4:12.

4. What was Titus to do for Zenas and Apollos? Briefly research Zenas and Apollos. What do Scripture and history tell us about them?

5. Why would Paul go to Nicopolis? Research to find out what this city was known for.

6. In the midst of Paul's words of farewell, what did he tell Titus in 3:14? Define *learn 3129*.

7. When do urgent needs arise? How can you learn to be prepared for the unexpected?

8. What are examples of *cases of urgent needs*? What have been urgent needs that your church has faced?

9. What is the result of failing to learn to be devoted to good works? Define *unfruitful 175*.

10. How can an older woman teach a younger woman to be devoted to good works, so as to help in cases of urgent need, and not be unfruitful?

Part Four: Grace be With You All

1. Read Titus 3:15. What does the last verse in Titus indicate about the church community in Crete?

2. How do church members develop love for one another?

3. What is your personal testimony about growing in love and relationships with your church members?

4. What do you learn about church order from Titus 3:1-15?

5. Read from commentary resources for information regarding the letter to Titus.

6. Reflect on all that you have studied in this letter to Titus. Write a testimony for an older or younger Cretan woman coming out of darkness and into God's marvelous light. Creatively use Titus chapter 3 for a guide to writing how God saved her. Write her salvation testimony.

    a. What was this woman like prior to salvation?

b. What was her name? Be creative and give her a name so you can personalize a testimony for her.

c. What changed this Cretan woman's life (Titus 2:11-14 and 3:4-8)? How did God save her?

d. Describe her new life in Christ. How is she becoming a godly woman? What are her good works? How does she view her local church? How did she respond to Titus's exhortations? How does she learn to be devoted to good works?

Part Five: Dear Paul

1. Write a reply letter or email back to the Apostle Paul. Use your imagination and ask him any outstanding questions you may have that were left unanswered. What would you thank him for? Be sure to appropriately date the letter.

2. Recall who delivered Paul's letter to the Philippians; whom would you ask to deliver your letter back to Paul?

Sophron Studies ⫷⫷

God in Titus

In-Class Worksheet

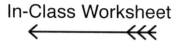

1. Review what you learned about God from the letter to Titus.

2. Use the chart below to describe God, according to the categories of each column.

His character	What He did	How or Why He did it

His character	What He did	How or Why He did it

Review and Reflection

Lesson Ten: Titus 1:1-3:15

Let them not escape from your sight;
keep them within your heart.

—Proverbs 4:21

Part One: Review

> *Don't rush through the questions this week, take time to read and review your previous nine weeks of homework! This is where context becomes most obvious and you see the letter as a whole.*
>
>

1. Read Titus chapters one through three. What are your impressions of this letter to Titus? Compare your answer with your original answer in Lesson One, Part One.

2. What are the repeated words and themes in this letter?

3. Describe the purpose of Paul's letter to Titus.

4. What were some of the issues in the Cretan churches?

5. What does it mean to *set in order*? Describe in detail all that Titus had to set in order.

6. List the qualifications for elder.

7. Describe the Cretans' spiritual maturity.

8. Where was Paul when he wrote the letter to Titus?

9. How did you most closely relate to the Cretans?

10. Recall the initial instructions to Titus in chapter one. How do Paul's instructions set up a framework for the entire letter?

Part Two: The Gospel in Titus

1. What was Titus to declare and insist upon to the Cretans?

2. Describe the purpose of believers *preaching the gospel* to themselves daily.

3. What does a gospel-centered church look like?

4. How are Christians to respond to people who behave like Cretans? How is the church to be involved in the world? How is the world to recognize that Christians are godly?

5. What do believers' good works say to those outside the church?

6. How were the false teachers putting the gospel at risk?

7. What was Titus to do with those opposing sound doctrine?

8. How have you experienced Jesus Christ and His gospel working through you during your study of Titus?

9. In what do believers hope? What is the future of those who have been saved (Titus 1: 2, 2:13, and 3:7)?

10. How are we to display the gospel?

Part Three: The Titus Mandate

1. Describe what is expected of a godly, older woman.

2. Describe what is expected of a godly, younger woman.

3. What does it mean for the older woman to *train* the younger woman?

4. Explain the Titus 2:3-5 mandate.

5. Why is the Titus 2:3-5 mandate to women important?

6. How do women influence the word of God?

7. How are we to become godly women (Titus 1:1-2 and 2:11-14)?

8. How is the reverent woman likened to a priest?

9. Where should a woman's good works have first priority?

10. What truth has convicted you the most about the Titus 2:3-5 mandate?

Part Four: Church Leadership

1. Where does leadership begin?

2. Why is biblical leadership essential to the church?

3. Explain how sound doctrine is critical to church leadership.

4. For what should the church be striving?

5. How does a woman influence church leadership?

6. How does Jesus Christ enable believers to be unified in His church body?

7. Why is church leadership important to those outside the church?

8. How did the letter to Titus help you better relate to your own church body?

9. Describe the efforts that must be made to be engaged in a discipleship relationship.

10. How was this study most encouraging to you?

Part Five: Sound Doctrine, Sound Thinking, Sound Living

1. Read Titus chapters one through three once more.

2. Complete the following worksheet.

SOUND DOCTRINE... SOUND THINKING... SOUND LIVING

The tagline for Sophron Studies is *Sound Doctrine…Sound Thinking…Sound Living*. These are the desired goals of inductive Bible study. It is God's word that dwells in our hearts to generate an intimate knowledge of our Savior, leading to godliness, which influences our lives toward right living.

1. Read through Titus, chapter by chapter and complete the chart below.

2. Note how each chapter presents sound doctrine, which then leads to sound thinking, and then, how this is lived out... soundly in our individual lives, within the local church.

Titus	Sound Doctrine	Sound Thinking	Sound Living
Chapter One			

Titus	Sound Doctrine	Sound Thinking	Sound Living
Chapter Two			
Chapter Three			

For the Sake of The Faith

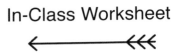

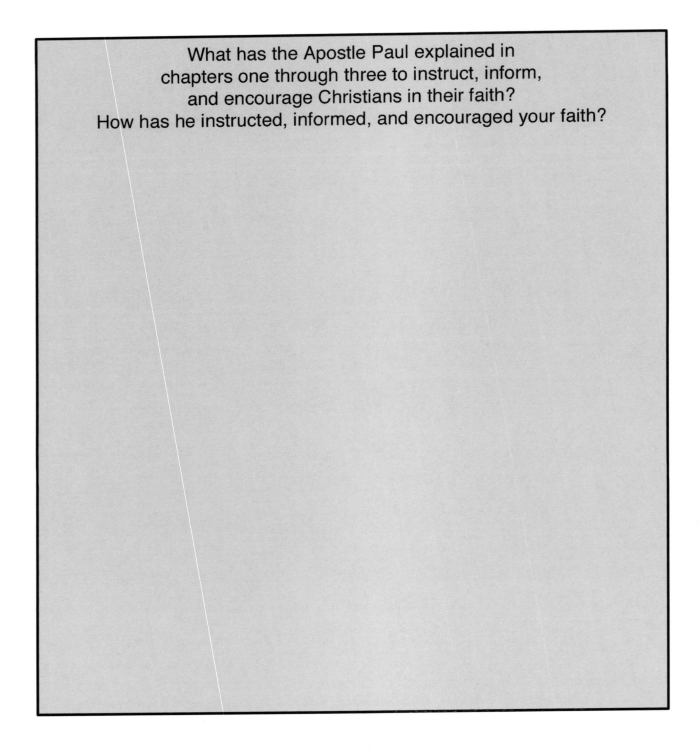

What has the Apostle Paul explained in
chapters one through three to instruct, inform,
and encourage Christians in their faith?
How has he instructed, informed, and encouraged your faith?

Lost in Translation

(Guideline to Word Studies)

There are many different modern-day language translations of the Bible. Which one is the best? Which version is the closest translation to the original language—Greek in the New Testament and Hebrew in the Old Testament? Is it true that some versions are better than others? All good questions! However, the fact remains: we are not reading Scripture in the language in which it was written. It is for this reason that it is often helpful to look at the original Greek or Hebrew word penned by the author.

For most of us, we have likely not attended or graduated from seminary, where we would be taught Hebrew, Greek, and etymology (the study of the origin of words). Therefore, it can be beneficial to look up the Greek or Hebrew words to aid in accurate interpretation.

If doing a word study seems intimidating, you can choose to simply read the passage you are studying in several different versions. We are not discounting the painstaking expertise of scholars and translators who have worked on the various versions of Scripture that we have available to us. We use many good resources to aid us in our word studies as well as our study; however, these resources do not take the place of the inspired Word of God and are not equal to the inspired Word of God. The Holy Spirit is our teacher (Luke 12:12; John 6:45, 14:26; Jeremiah 31:34).

Now we have received not the spirit of the world,
but the Spirit who is from God,
that we might understand the things freely given us by God.

1 Corinthians 2:12

A simple way to do a word study is to use the website blueletterbible.org.

• Choose the passage you are studying and tap or click on the verse.

• Then tap or click on *Tools* and then *Interlinear*; note the verse in the original language.

- Scroll down and the verse will be shown in the transliteration version (the change of a word from original Greek or Hebrew into the English letters of our alphabet) along with the Strong's Concordance number. The Strong's number is from the *Strong's Exhaustive Concordance of the Bible,* also known as *Strong's Concordance. Strong's Concordance* is an exhaustive cross-reference of every word in the King James Version. It is *not* a commentary, but a cross-reference tool.

- Tap or click on the Greek or Hebrew transliteration to see a definition.

Example of a Greek Word Study

> But Martha was distracted with much serving. And she went up to him and said, "Lord, do you not care that my sister has left me to serve alone? Tell her then to help me." But the Lord answered her, "Martha, Martha, you are anxious and troubled about many things, but one thing is necessary, Mary has chosen the good portion, which will not be taken away from her." (Luke 10:40–42, ESV)

Look at the word *distracted 4049.* As you work through this Bible study, the Greek or Hebrew word that you will be asked to define will always be italicized, followed by a Strong's number.

The Greek transliteration for *distracted* is *perispao,* and the definition is to draw different ways at the same time, hence to distract with cares and responsibilities. To be driven about mentally. Figuratively it means to be drawn around in the mind, preoccupied. Synonym: anxious. Antonyms: to take heed, to exercise thought.

God says, "Think over what I say, for the Lord will give you understanding in everything" (2 Timothy 2:7). Word studies can cause us to think, reflect, meditate, and consider what God says in a verse that we are studying. For example, you could ask the Holy Spirit to show you what easily distracts you? When am I drawn in different ways, at the same time, the context being things of this world that may keep me from the important things of God's world?

Is it necessary to do word studies for proper interpretation? No. However, it can be useful for clarity, understanding, and further study. Additionally, it is helpful to look at the synonyms and antonyms for further meaning.

As a final note, we *do not* do word studies to have superior speech or wisdom (1 Corinthians 2:1). We have nothing to boast about except the Lord. We want to say like the Apostle Paul, "I have decided to know nothing among you except Jesus Christ and Him crucified."

Recommended Resources

https://www.blueletterbible.com/

http://www.biblestudytools.com/

https://www.biblegateway.com/

http://www.biblestudytools.com/concordances/strongs-exhaustive-concordance/